*A Mark Dahle Portfolio*

# Derrack's Folly

## *Present Divestment #5*

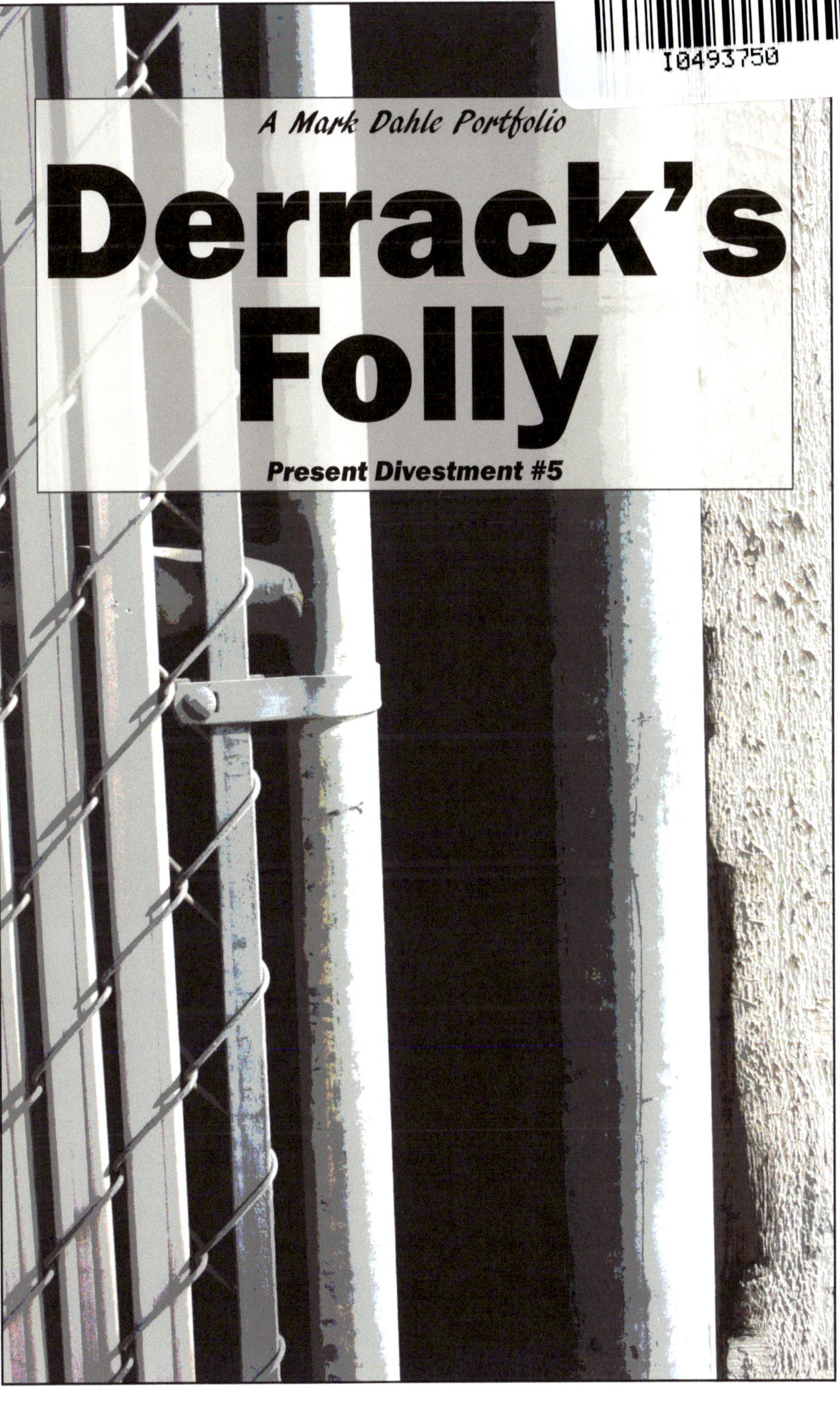

*Mark Dahle Portfolios can be read in a few minutes and enjoyed for a lifetime.*

*This portfolio includes the fifth story in the Present Divestment series, a photo of a beautiful 36 x 24 inch painting (at the right) and twenty-six slightly altered photographs.*

*Unlike many picture books, the text is unrelated to the paintings and photographs. This might seem weird at first. One thing that helps is to order more portfolios until you get used to it.*

*Photographs in this book are available in limited editions. See http://www.MarkDahle.com for more information and for previews of upcoming portfolios.*

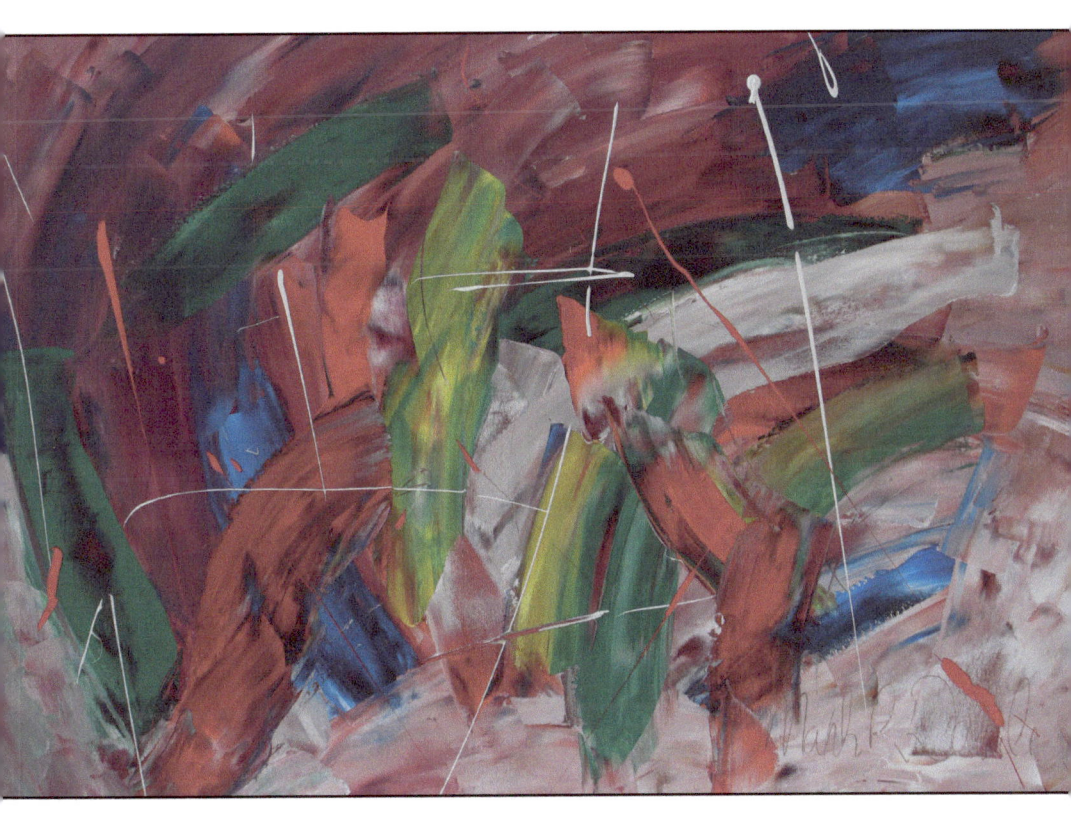

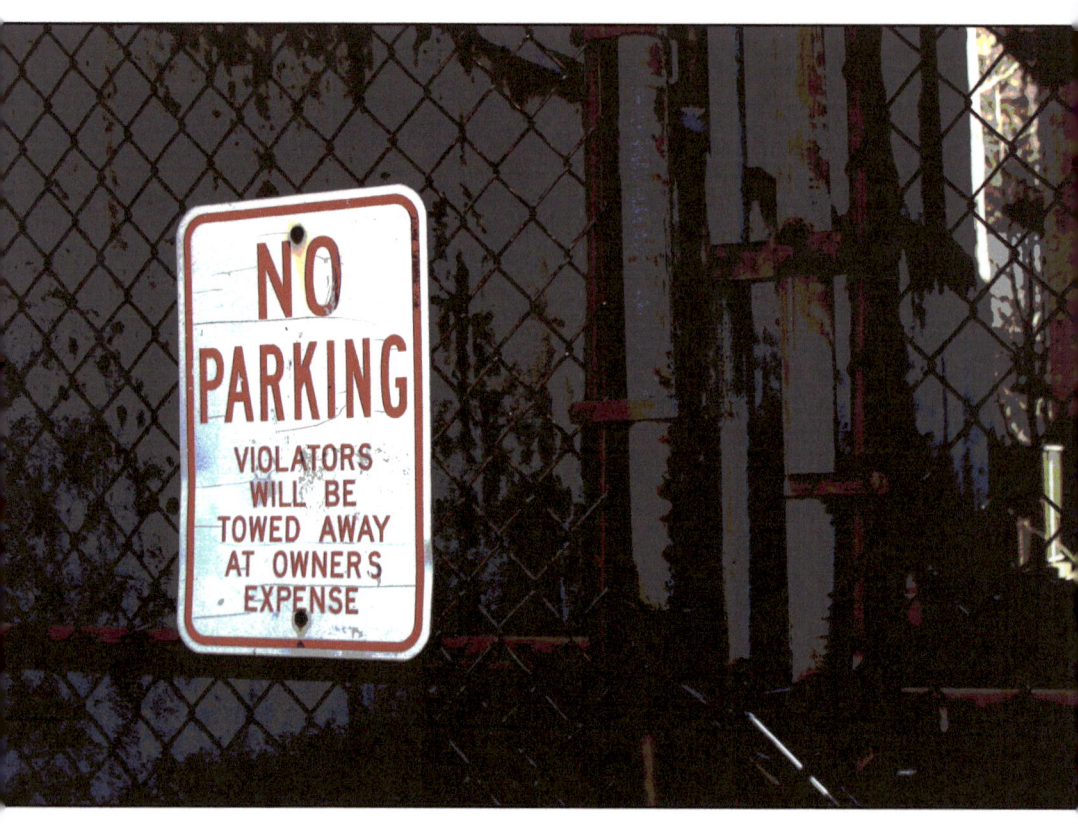

Lisa would have done what J-rex suggested even without hyptrolysis. She loved him. She trusted him. But at this point, that didn't matter. The hyptrolysis was directing her actions: She and the kids needed to scramble like they were at level ten. She shook her head. Level ten! How was that even possible? But she followed the command.

Lisa had her AutoCab head for the school without delay. She was shaking, so it was good she didn't have to drive. *Ten!* Everything in the plant wiped out, erased. All the files, all the equipment, all the programs, all the buildings. Whatever J-rex was dealing with was bad, bad, bad. She hoped he'd survive. She tried not to think about life without him.

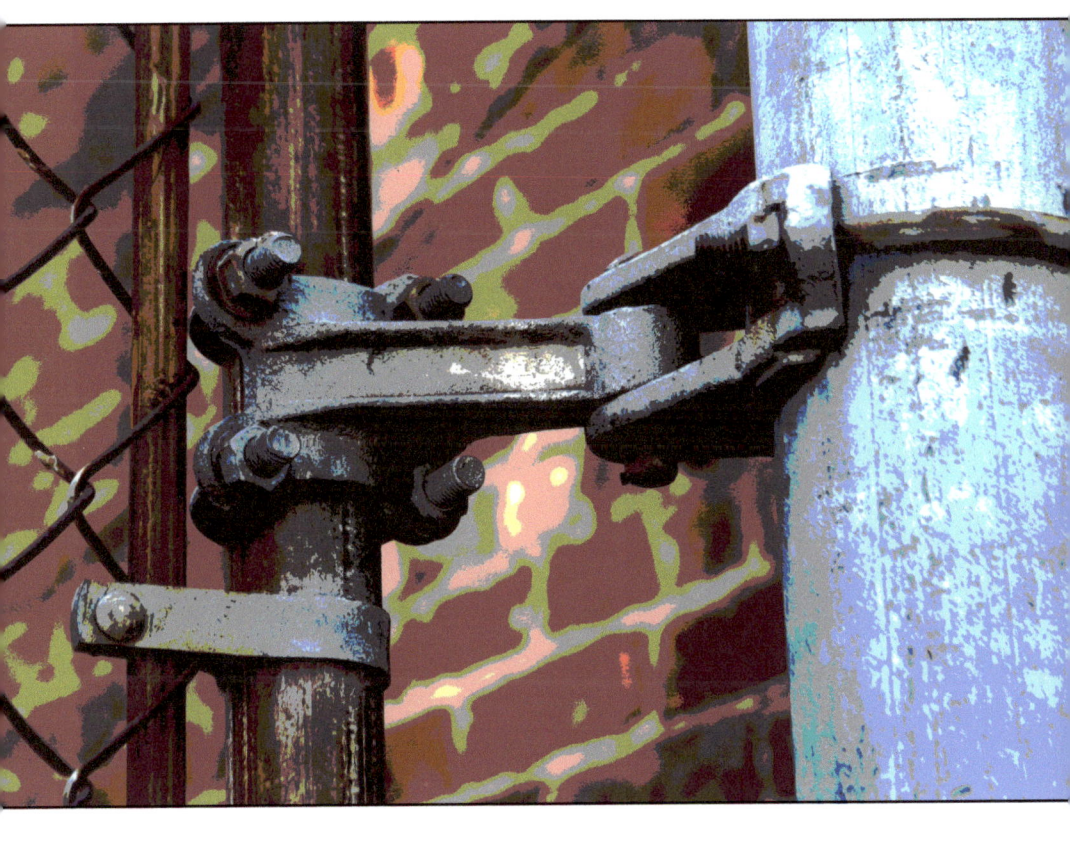

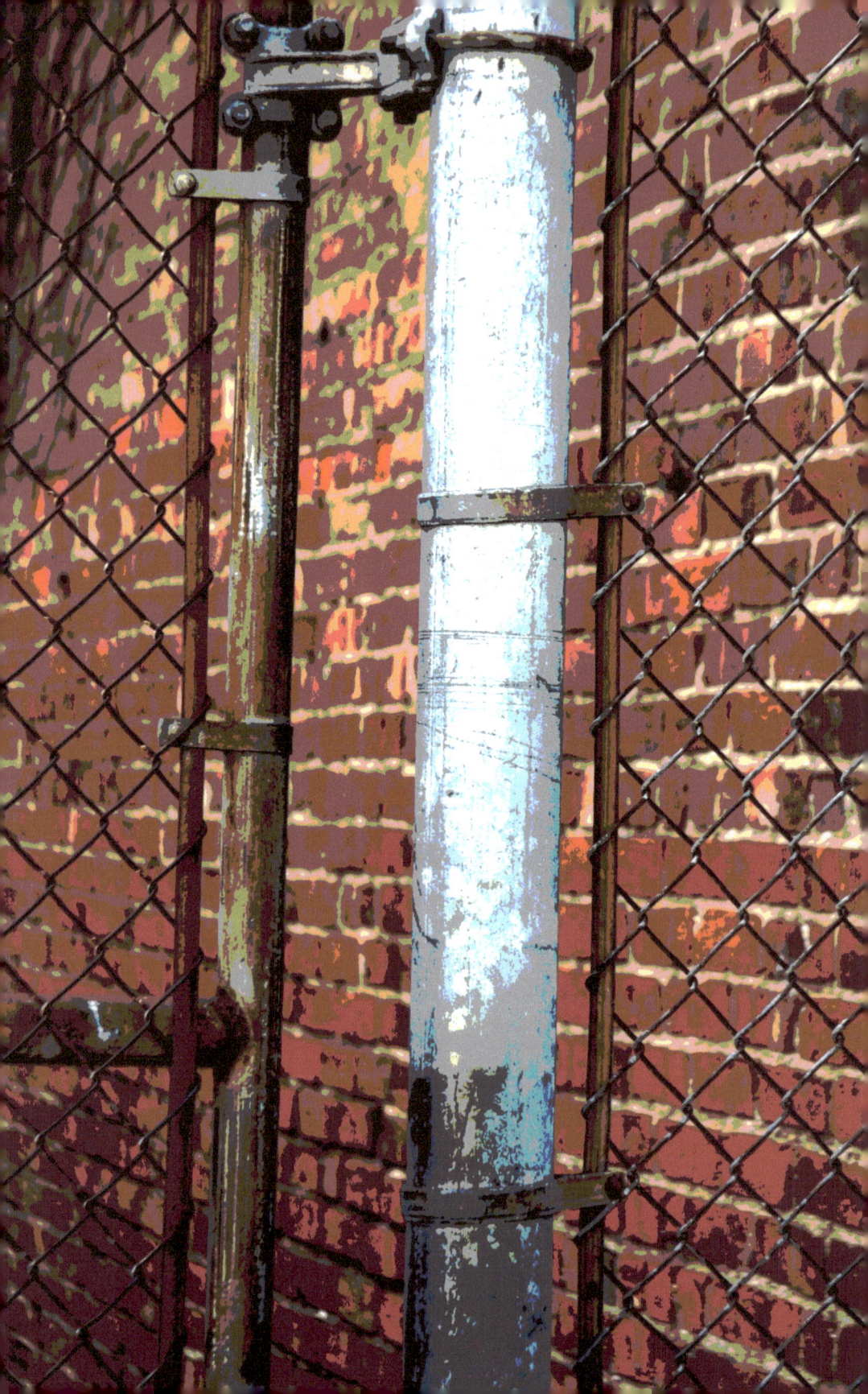

Lisa forced herself to think about her present task. She needed to be sharp. The Corporation was going to nine. She would have to move fast. Key people would evacuate, and insiders would notice.

Almost all the insiders at the Corporation had said to at least one person (against all protocol): "Look, I'm not supposed to tell you this. But this is a list of six names. If you ever hear about any three of them leaving on the same day, you get out of town as fast as you can. Don't wait, don't think, don't delay. And get as far away as you can. I can't tell you more."

Almost everyone who was told this paid attention, because the people who told them *never* joked about security matters – and rarely said anything else about their jobs at the Corporation.

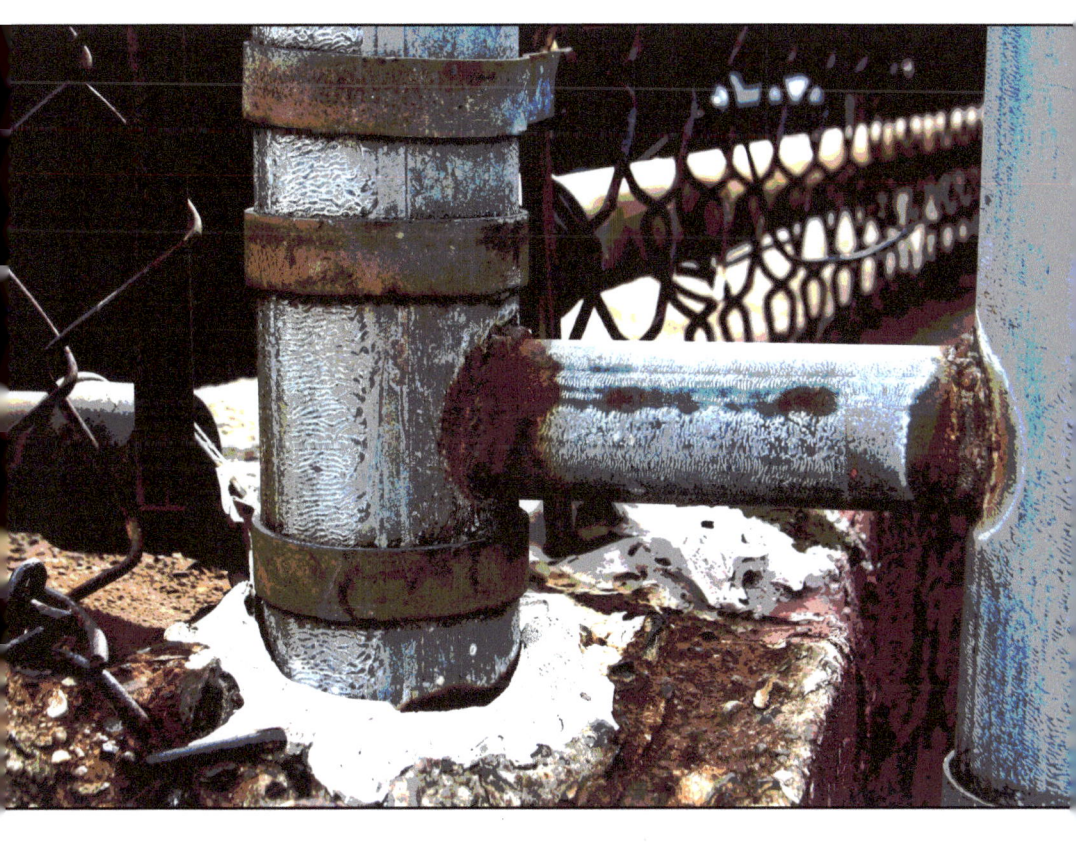

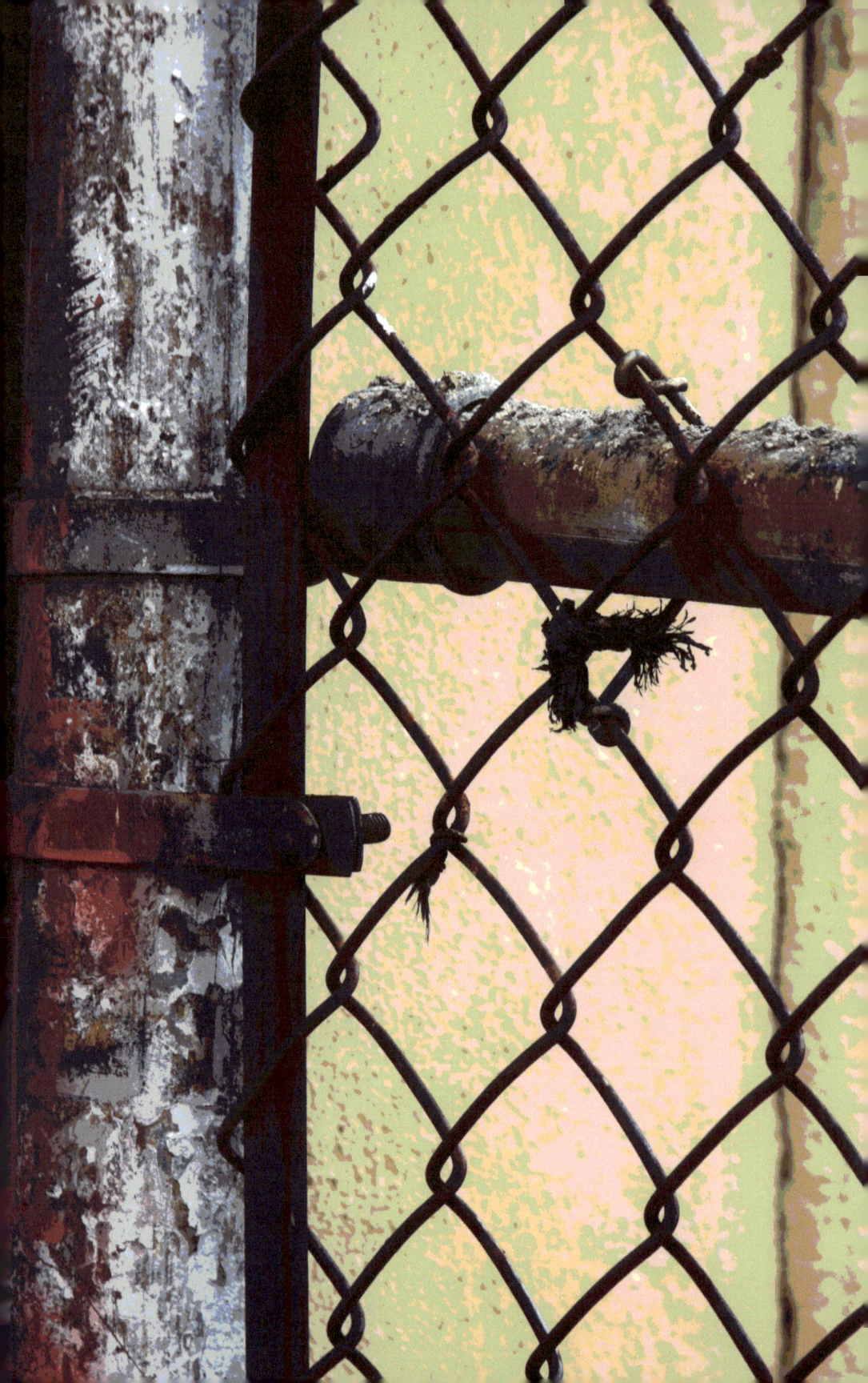

J-rex had told Lisa more than others had, partly because he had thought more about it. He also had more data to work with.

"If an evacuation starts," he had told her, "most of the general public won't notice, at first. But there's about 500 of us at the Corporation that will be called into the fire. That's 500 people who know what the levels are, at least up to nine. Suppose they each have made plans for their families to silently evacuate if they get called in. That's 500 kids or more leaving school on the same day, at about the same time, with 500 care givers and spouses crowding the school office to pick them up, pretending not to be panicked. There's no way that'll work. Who knows what kind of alarms that will set off. So here's the point: You'll have to be one of the first. My guess? By the time a school has had twenty parents showing up with a 'family emergency,' they'll start to ask questions and slow the process way down. The school may even put itself on lockdown, and then *nobody* will get out. There's only one way around it: You have to be one of the first."

J-rex had also thought about the airport and train. "If you get out early, take the first plane *anywhere* off the continent. But if you get delayed, there may be hundreds at the airport looking for a flight. If you're lucky, the others won't know to get as far away as I'm telling you. But if everyone's trying to get on the next international flight, it will trigger the government AnomalyAlert, and then everything will be shut down. If that happens, don't stay at the airport waiting for the alert to end. It won't happen. Get on the BulletTrain or take a bus to the HeloPort – anything – just keep getting as far away as you can, and don't stop until you've crossed an ocean."

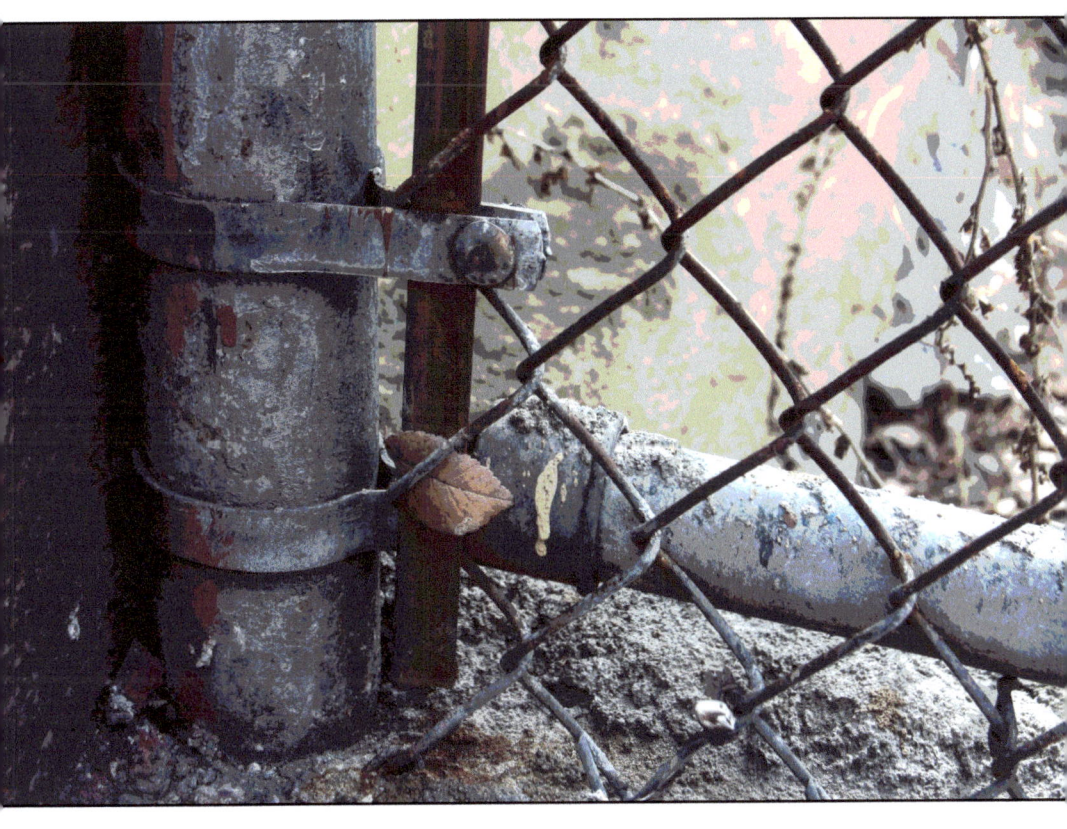

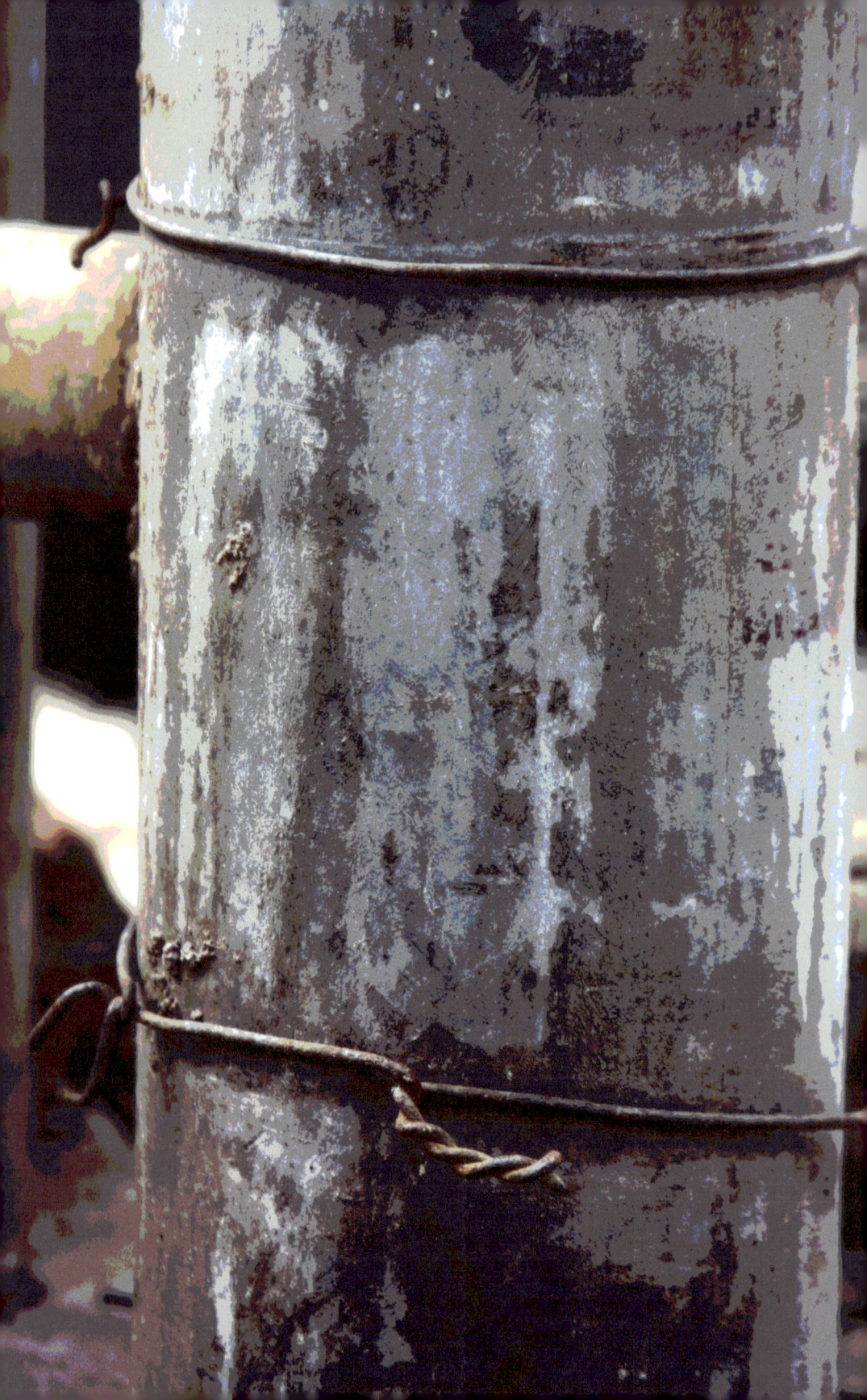

Thinking about her need to be one of the first at the school, Lisa instructed the AutoCab to speed and began paying the tickets as they arrived.

When Lisa left, she'd grabbed Eli and Derrack's EmerKit as well as her own. They were always packed for a possible evacuation, even though she'd never thought one would come. She had left J-rex's EmerKit at the house, not knowing what else to do. If he had wanted her to bring it, surely he would have said so. She had reset the house to Vacation mode. Her own EmerKit didn't have much in the way of extra clothes, but she could always stop at a mall wherever they landed.

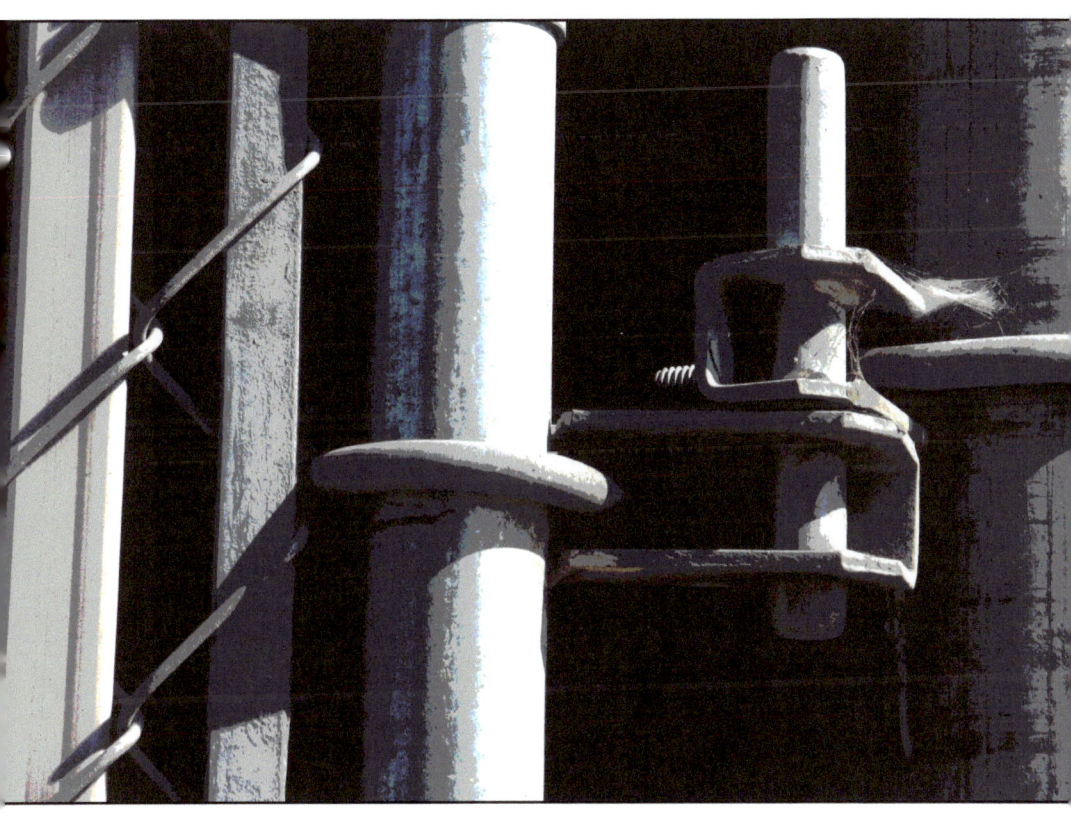

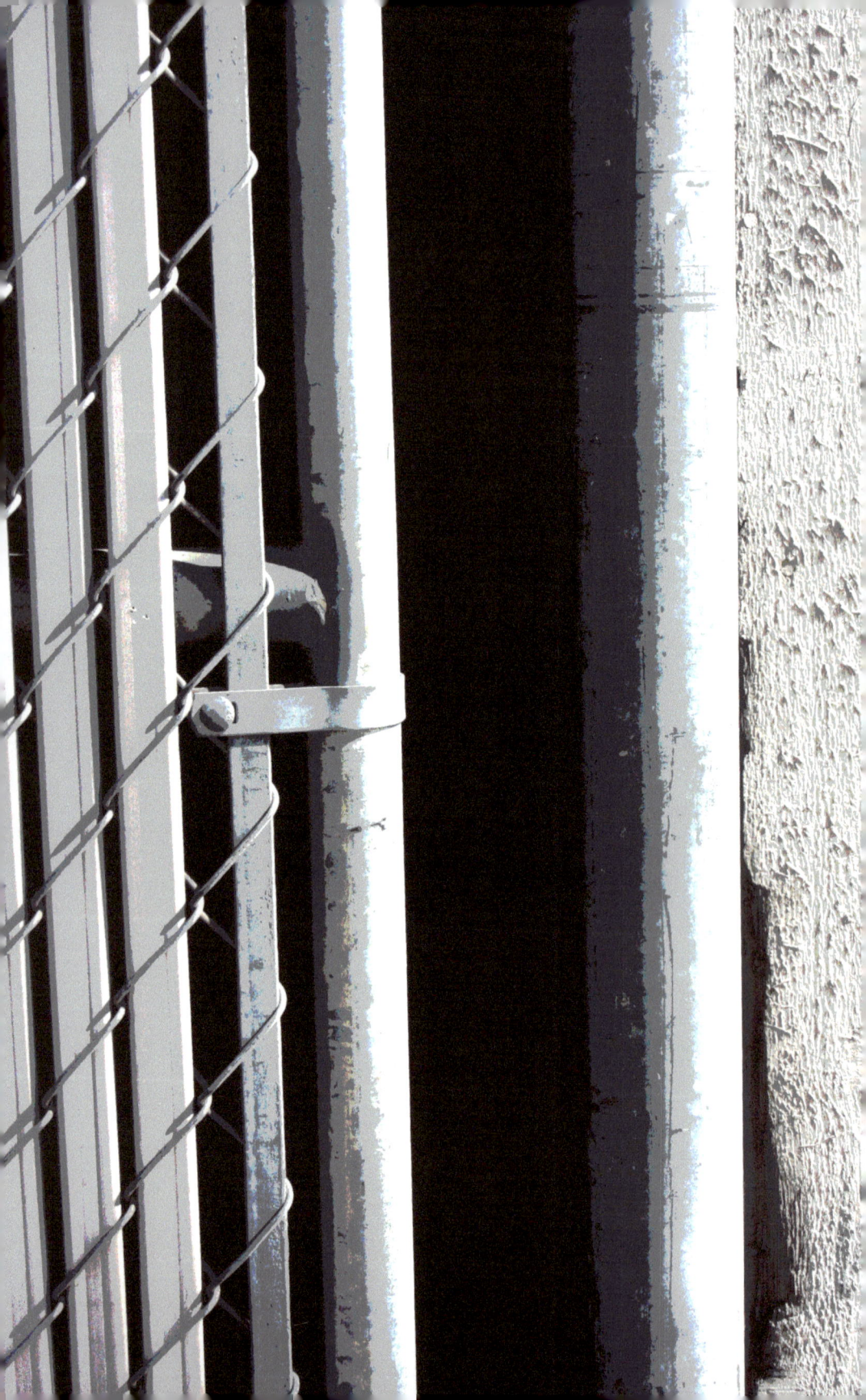

Lisa was still thinking through her plans when the NorthAm NewsFeed's weather forecast was interrupted. "The Senate's debate on Species Control ended early today, when the Vice President called for an unscheduled half-hour recess, followed by lunch, to give time for all sides to hammer out details of a compromise. Talks are scheduled to resume at 2 p.m. today, and if they *do* come to a compromise, we'll keep you informed of the breakthrough when it happens. Meanwhile, Senator Carl Gabbon has been excused due to a death in his family. He expects to be back tomorrow."

Lisa bit her lip. The Vice President and Gabbon were two of the six. If the Corporation was at level nine, some of the families who knew what the levels meant might become skittish.

Since Lisa knew they really should be at level ten, she was certain the Vice President would not return from lunch at 2 p.m. – this was just an excuse to give a few people the chance to slip away without being noticed.

Lisa had a long drive to the school; if too many people heard the news, she might not arrive early enough.

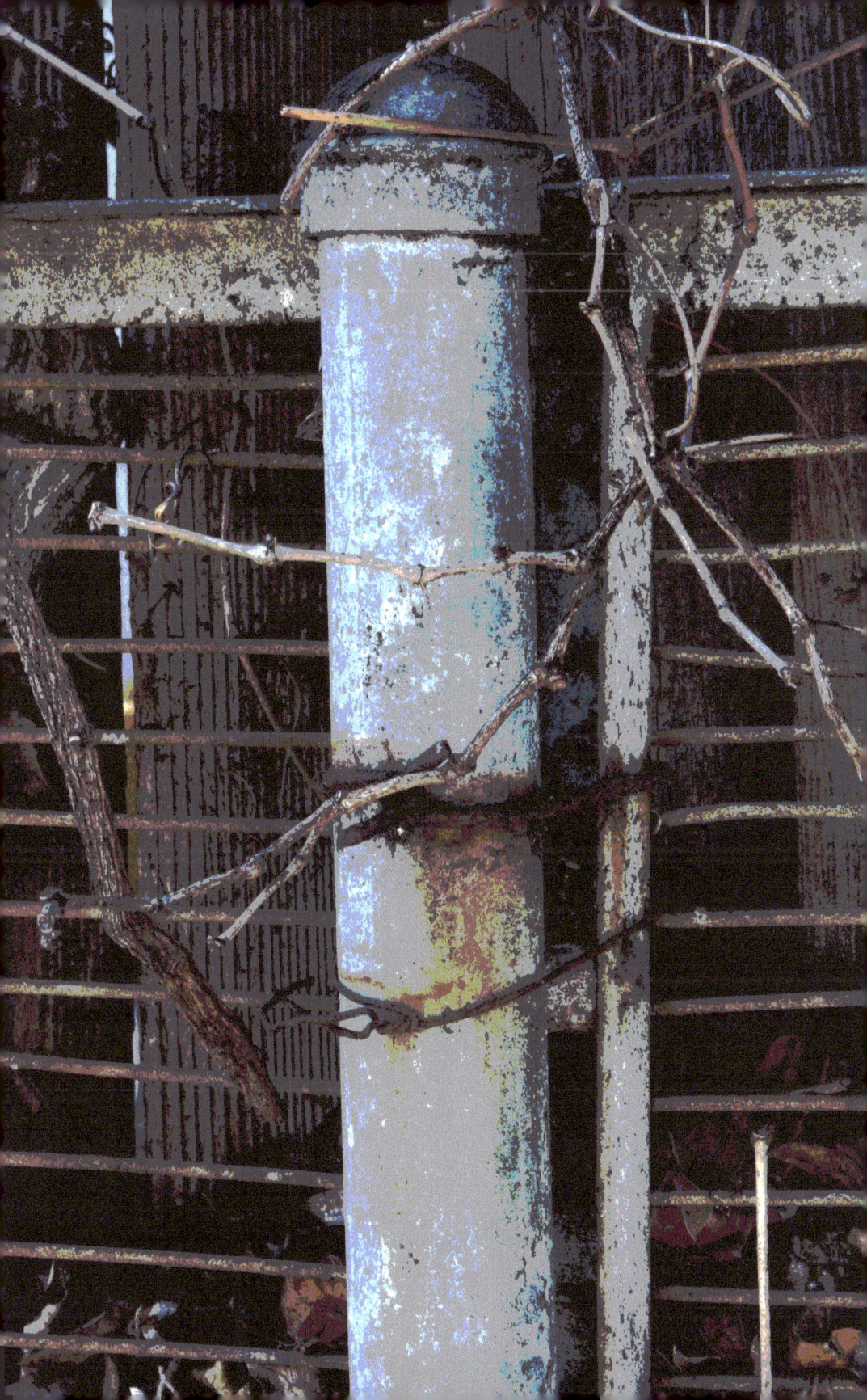

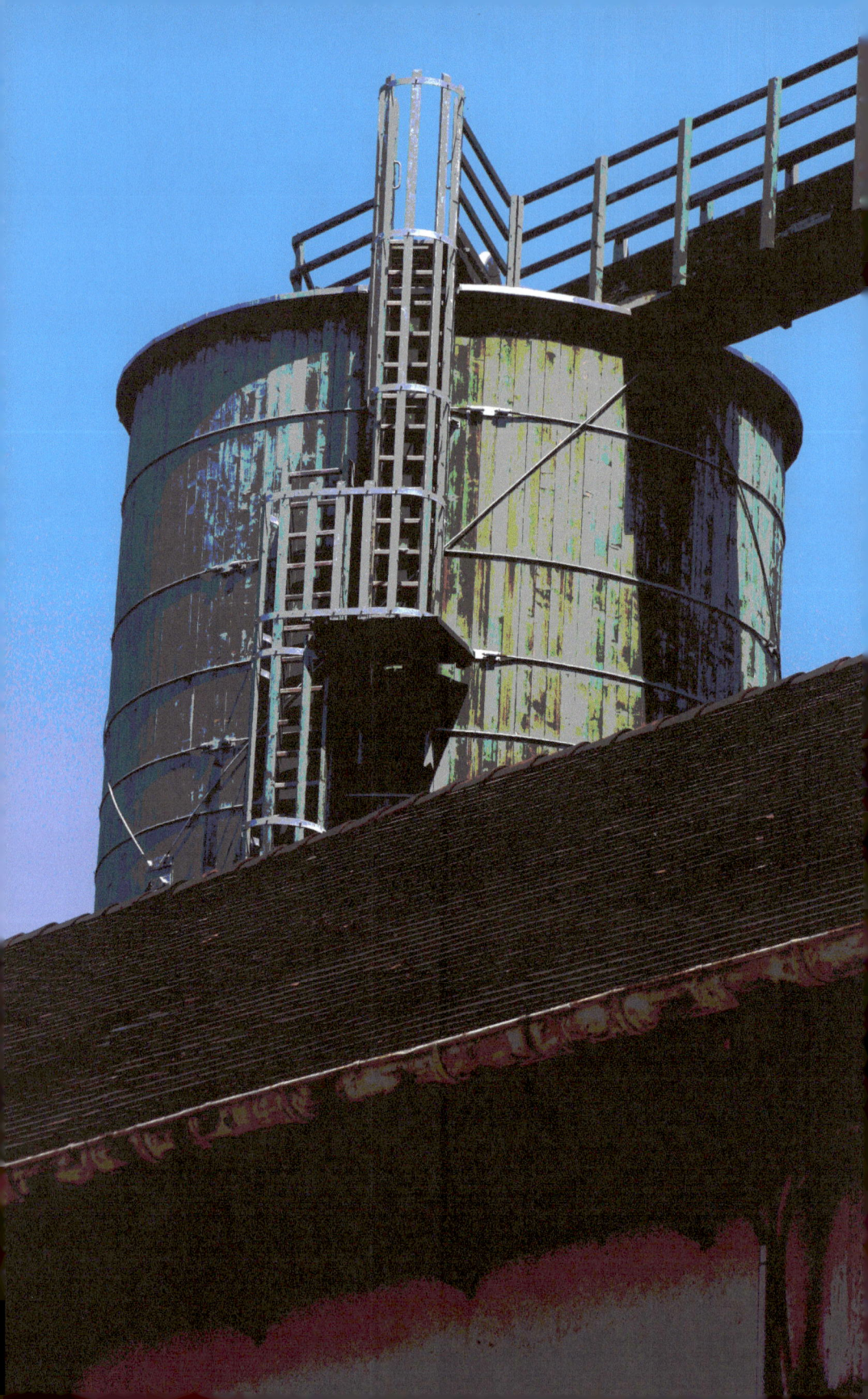

Lisa sent an InstaText to Eli and Derrack, telling them to meet her in the school's office because of a family emergency. She copied the principal.

Lisa turned on the CorpChannel to see if she could get any clues to what was going on at the Corporation. To her shock, she saw that the level had gone down from seven to five.

Five? She felt foolish. What if she took her kids out of school and flew to South America and there was no crisis? Maybe J-rex was so busy he just forgot to tell her everything was okay. Or maybe he couldn't call for some reason.

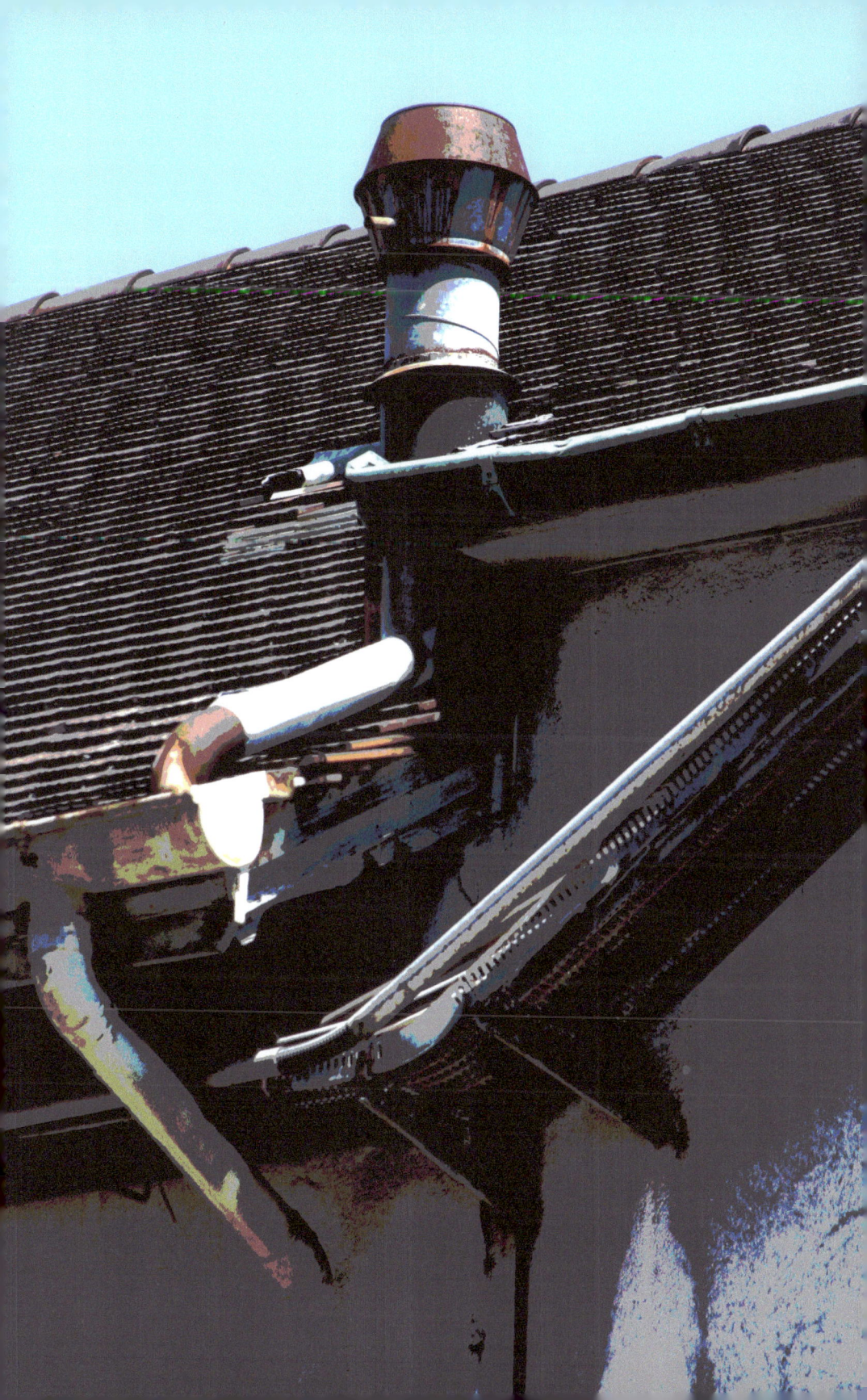

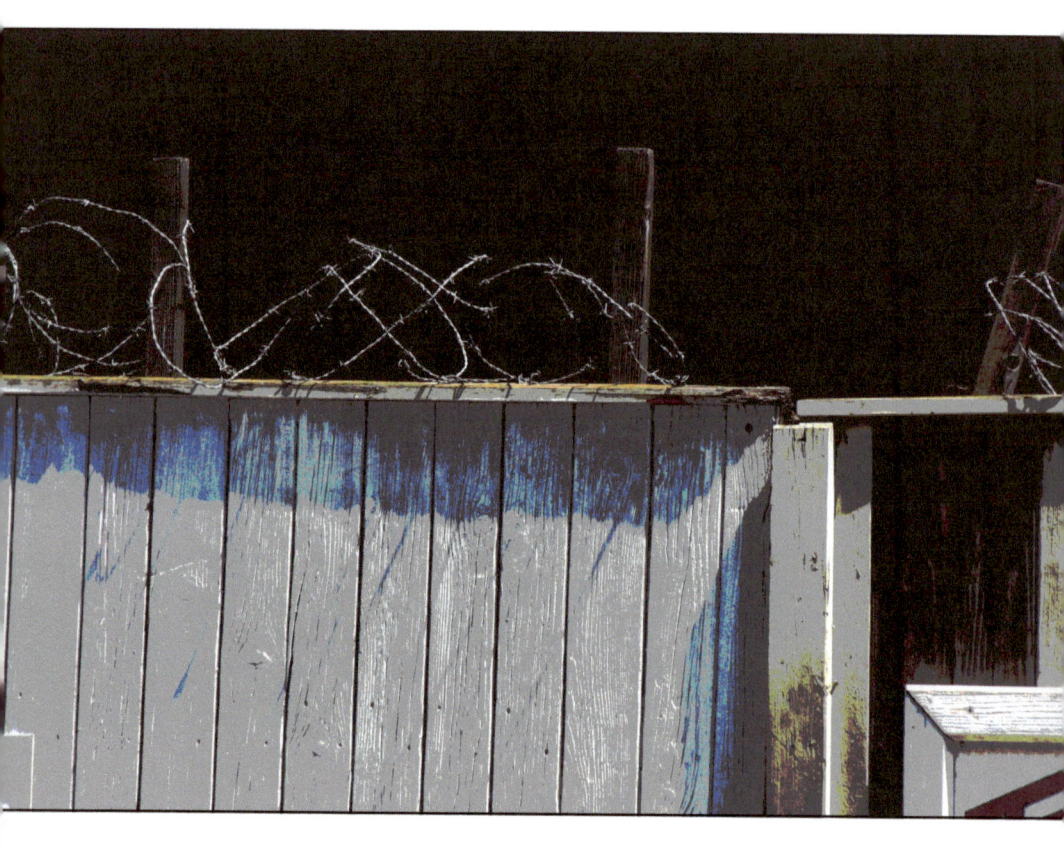

Lisa almost turned the AutoCab around and started back for home. Maybe she *would* have if she hadn't been under hyptrolysis. Then she figured it out. "It's just a ruse," she said to herself. "They're pretending everything's improving just so people don't pay attention to those who are leaving."

A second later, she realized that the falling status was to her advantage. She wouldn't have to worry about mobs of parents at school. Nobody would pay attention to an unscheduled Senate recess at level five. She had two and a half hours to get her kids on a plane before the Senate came back to session and people noticed some key Senators were absent. She smiled and relaxed. In five minutes she'd be at the school picking up her kids. This was going to be easy.

\*\*\*

When Derrack got the InstaText to go immediately to the school office, he was not on the school campus. He'd been skipping school for a month, using a ParentPass he'd hacked so he could test new products at ParthuCom's EnviroFeast. The Feast, for all its fancy advertising, was what in the 20th century would have been called a drug cartel, although this was a far more public version, made possible by the new laws. Derrack was at the Feast both because he was hooked and because he wanted to get into sales. He was competing to become the new rep for his class at school, and he had two days of training left to go.

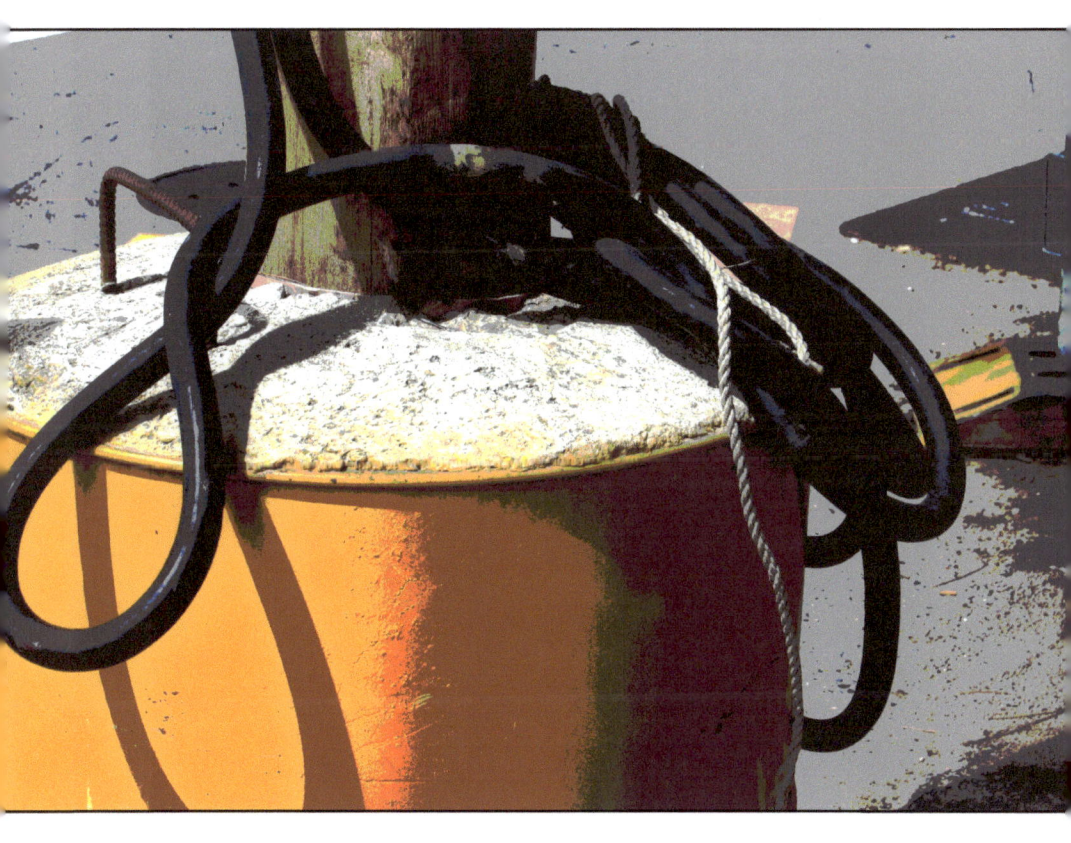

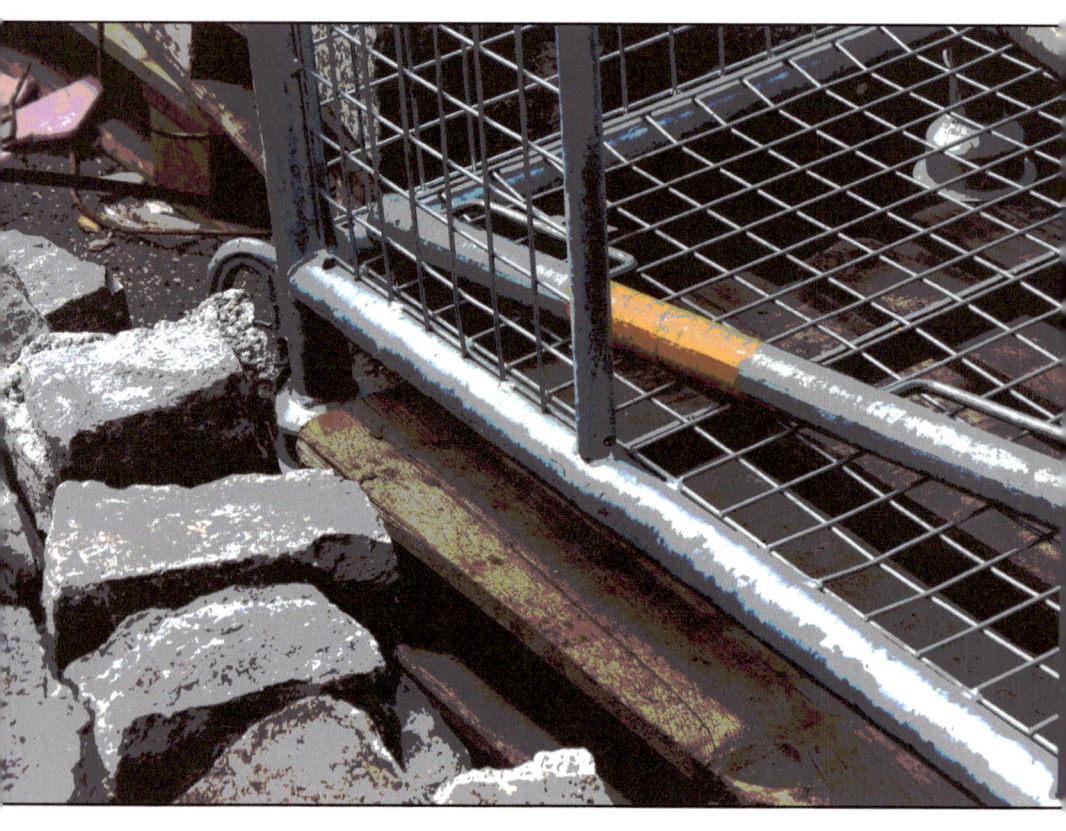

Derrack swore when he saw that the InstaText was copied to the principal. In a few minutes when his mom arrived, his ParentPass would be exposed as a forgery.

Derrack didn't want to leave training with only two days to go. He was so close to joining the sales team.

And then he realized he didn't need to leave. His cover was blown, or would be in a couple minutes. If he went back to school now, he'd trip the DrugDetect and probably wind up in jail. Then once he got out of jail he'd have to face his father. He wasn't going to do *that.*

No, whatever emergency caused his mom to drop by the school just forced his hand. He'd wanted to leave home anyway. Now he would.

\*\*\*

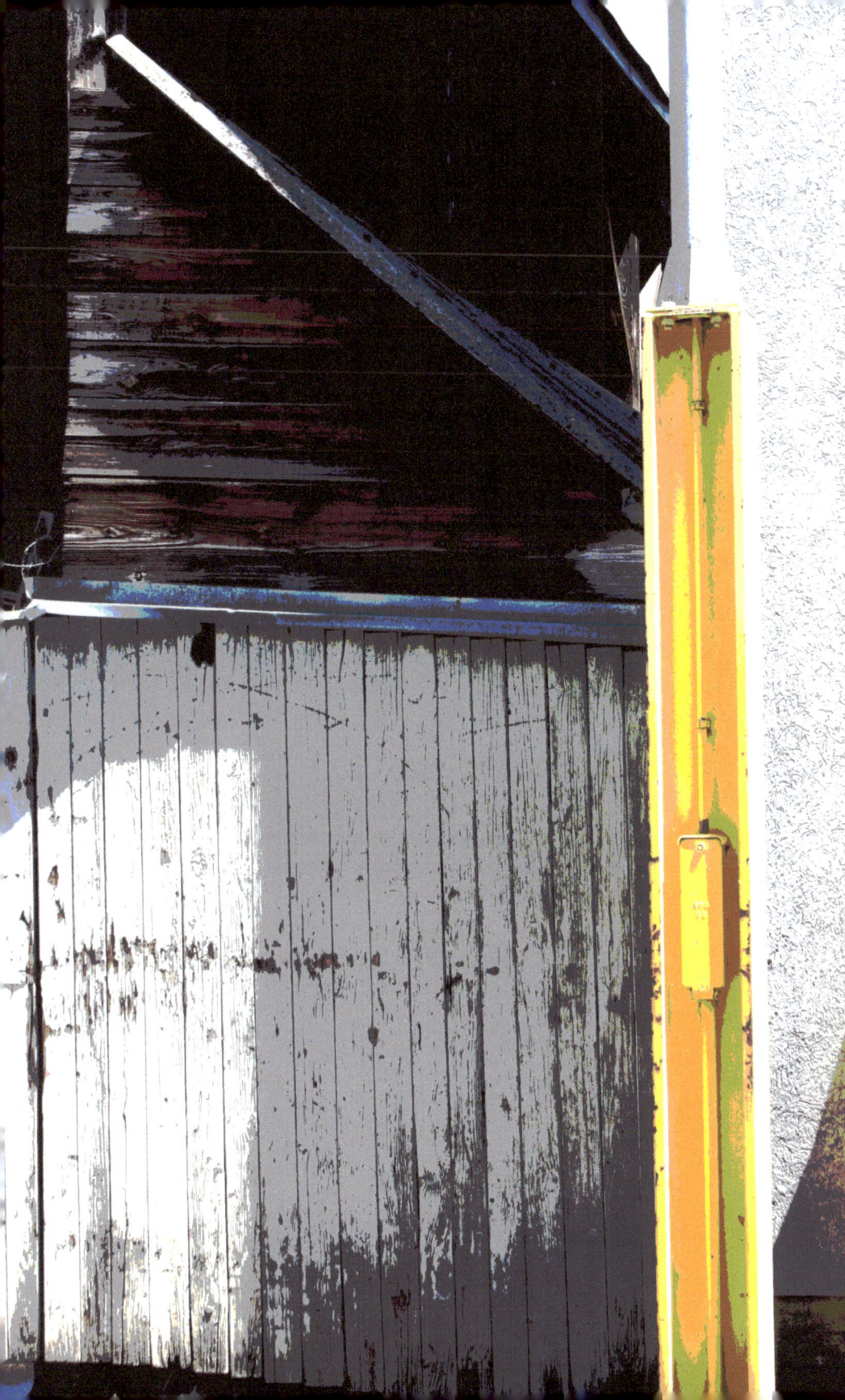

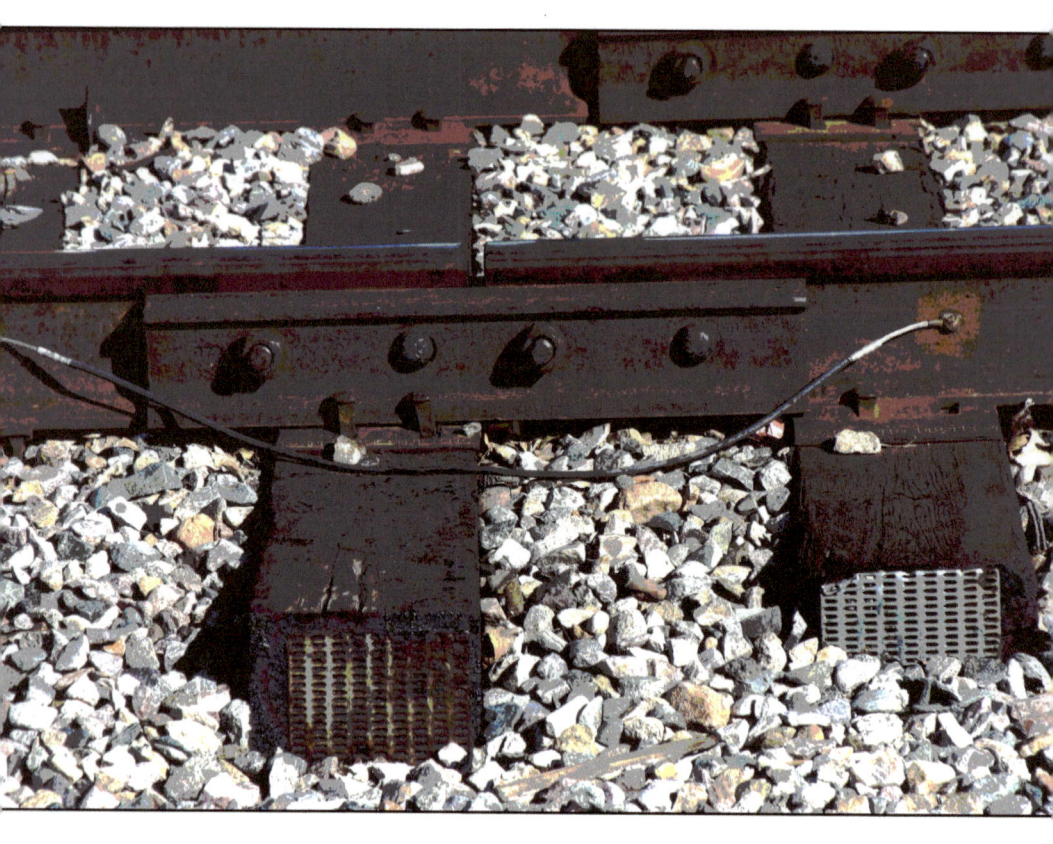

Eli was at the office when Lisa arrived. She had already put most of the contents of her locker in her pack. She knew a family emergency meant she might not be coming back, and there were plenty of things she didn't want to leave behind.

Lisa guessed Derrack would be there soon. She glanced around; only one other parent was in the office with an emergency. She desperately wanted to ask where he worked, to see if he was a Corporation employee. But she didn't want to arouse suspicion. And she had plenty of other things to worry about when the clerk told her Derrack had been gone all month, using a ParentPass that had her signature on it. Lisa tried hard not to look surprised at the news. She needed to get out without setting off any alarms. So she pretended that she knew about the pass, but had sent the text just to make sure the school records reported the family emergency for both kids.

She signed Eli out and left.

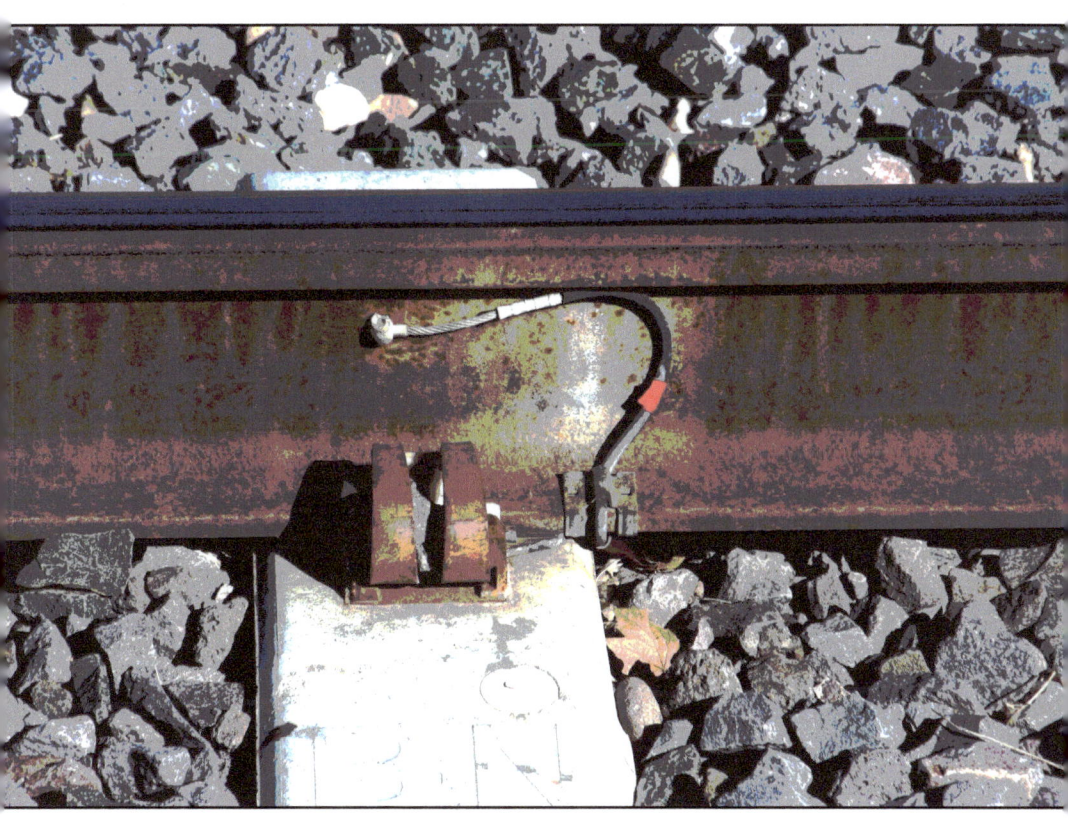

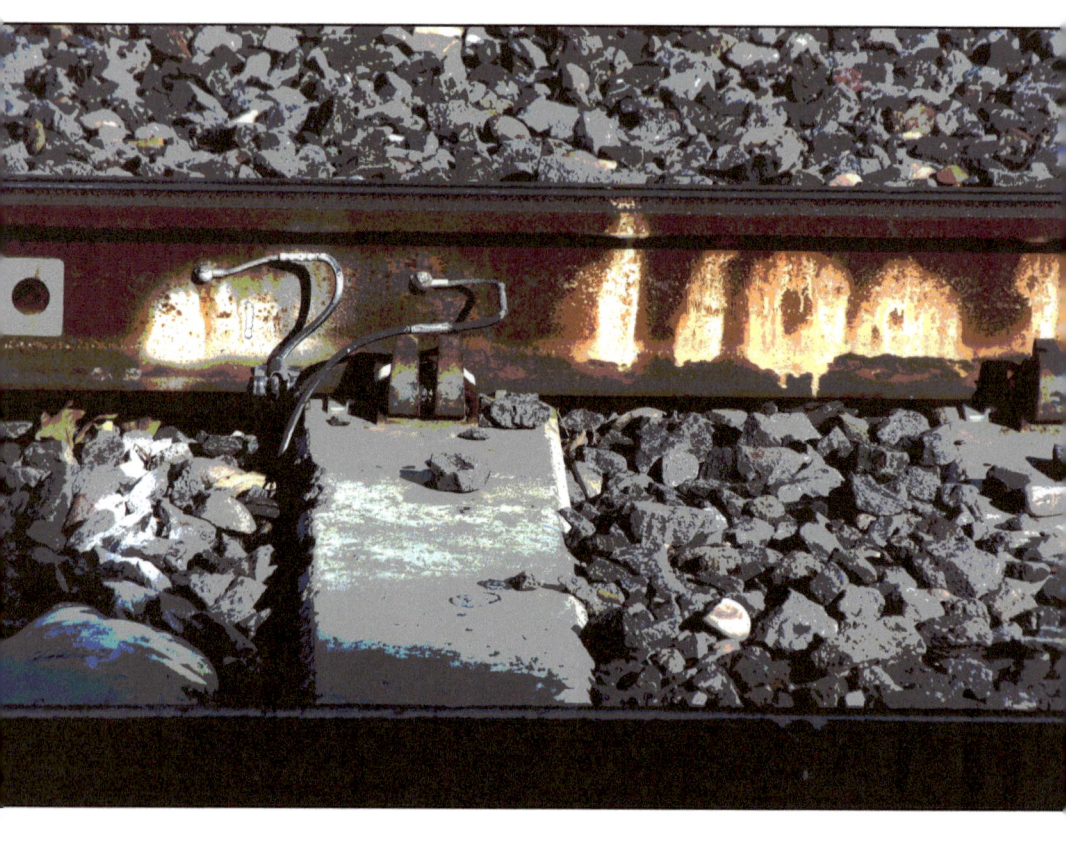

The part about the ParentPass having her signature was a problem. To get her signature, Derrack had to know her IdentiChipID. If he'd forged the ParentPass a month ago, who knows what else he had forged in the meantime. She'd have to check her CreditRecords fast and probably get a new ID.

But first she had to find Derrack. Where could he be? And what had he been doing for a month?

As Lisa left the office with Eli, two more students arrived, both holding InstaTexts. Lisa guessed that was more than a coincidence. Even though the Corporation was officially at level five, maybe the word was starting to spread.

"Do you know those kids?" Lisa whispered. "Do you know what their parents do?"

"They're both Corp brats. I've seen them at the annual picnic. Kelly's mom is a SecurPatrol. I think Jack's dad is on a MediCorp team."

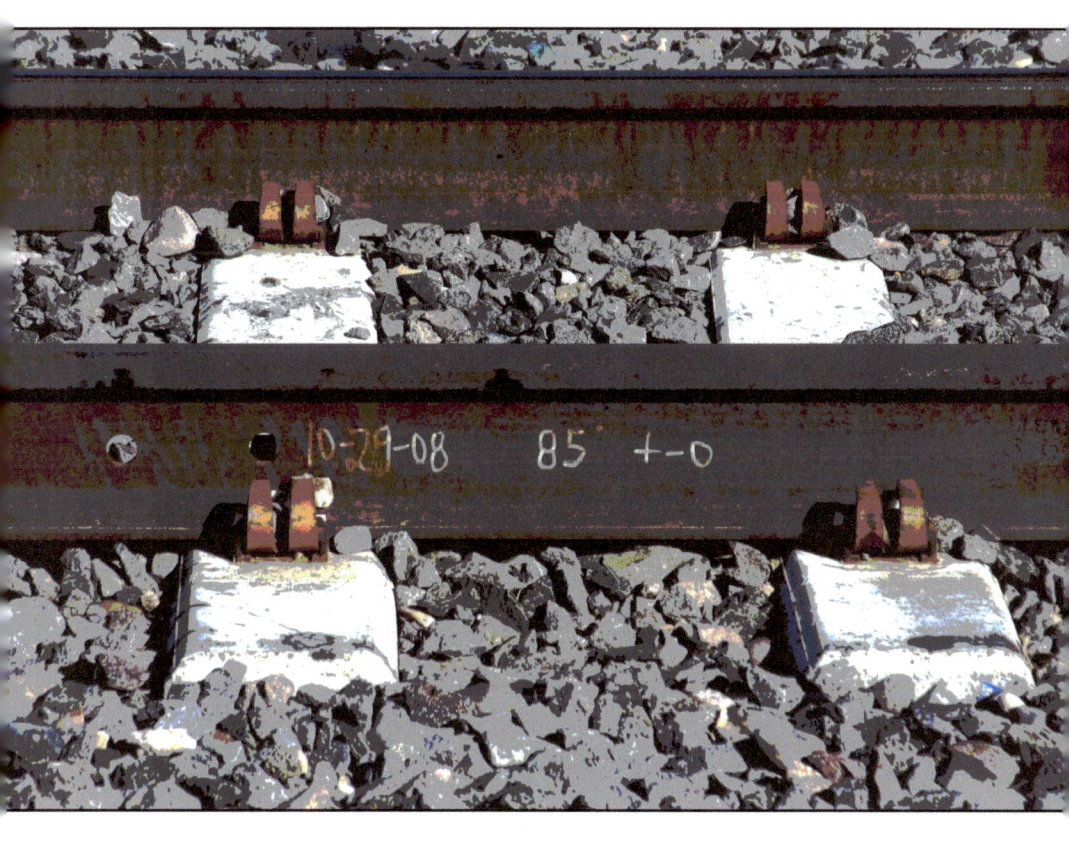

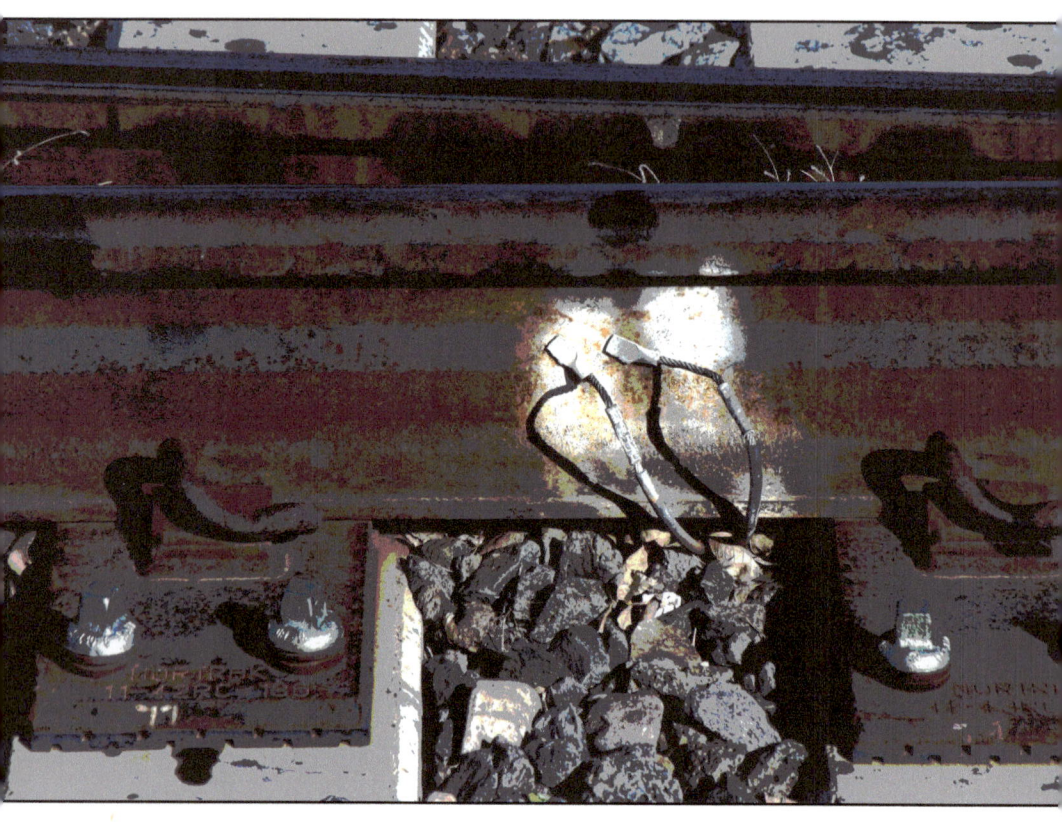

Lisa thought about it. It wasn't what she expected. These weren't the Corporation's officers' kids. These were the lower level firefighters getting their kids out. So maybe word wasn't completely out. The starting trickle was just from the people immediately involved with the trouble, maybe just the people on J-rex's teams. Maybe the bulk of the Corporation was still ignorant, thinking they were at level five.

"Any idea where your brother is?"

"He said he had a job interview."

"One that lasted a *month?* And one that required a forged pass?" Lisa frowned. She knew what that meant. She directed the AutoCab to head to the closest EnviroFeast.

\*\*\*

Derrack was just slipping into the ecstasy of a HyperLoop5 when he got the second InstaText from his mom. He had been expecting it. But he had expected her to ask where he was; all his phones were on SecurMode and his location couldn't be hacked, so he was confident she wouldn't know where to find him.

Instead the text said, "We're coming to pick you up at ten."

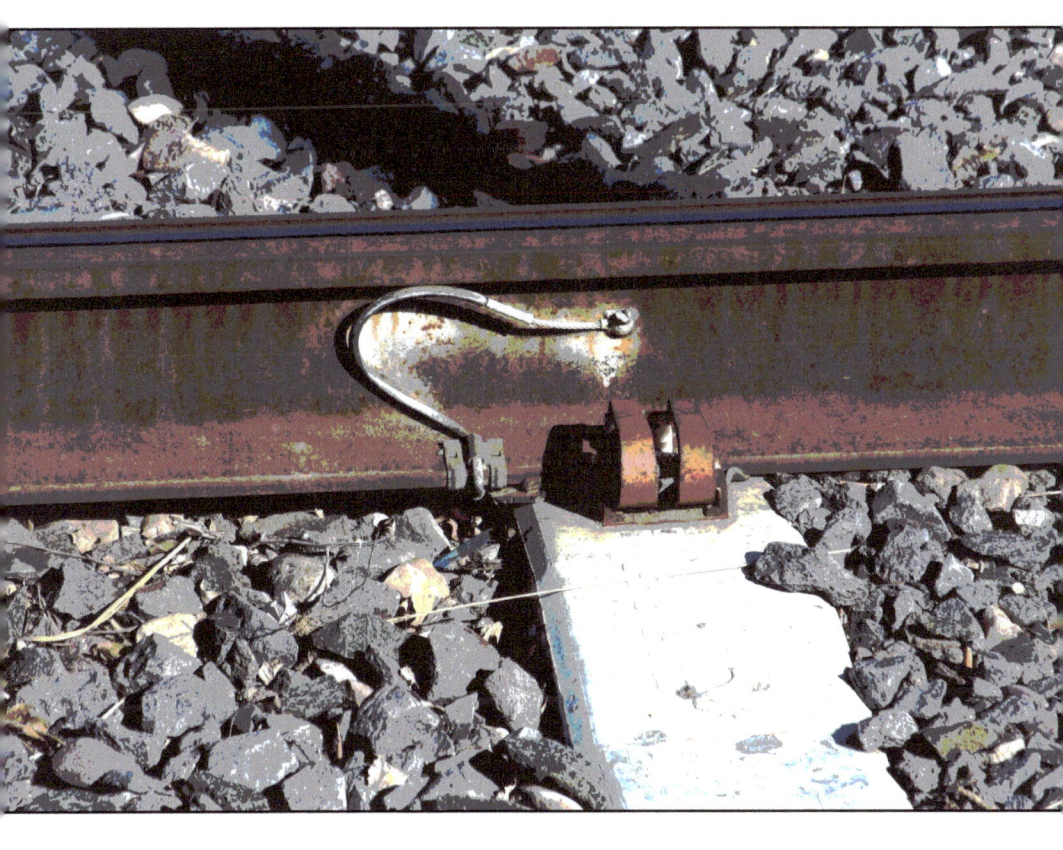

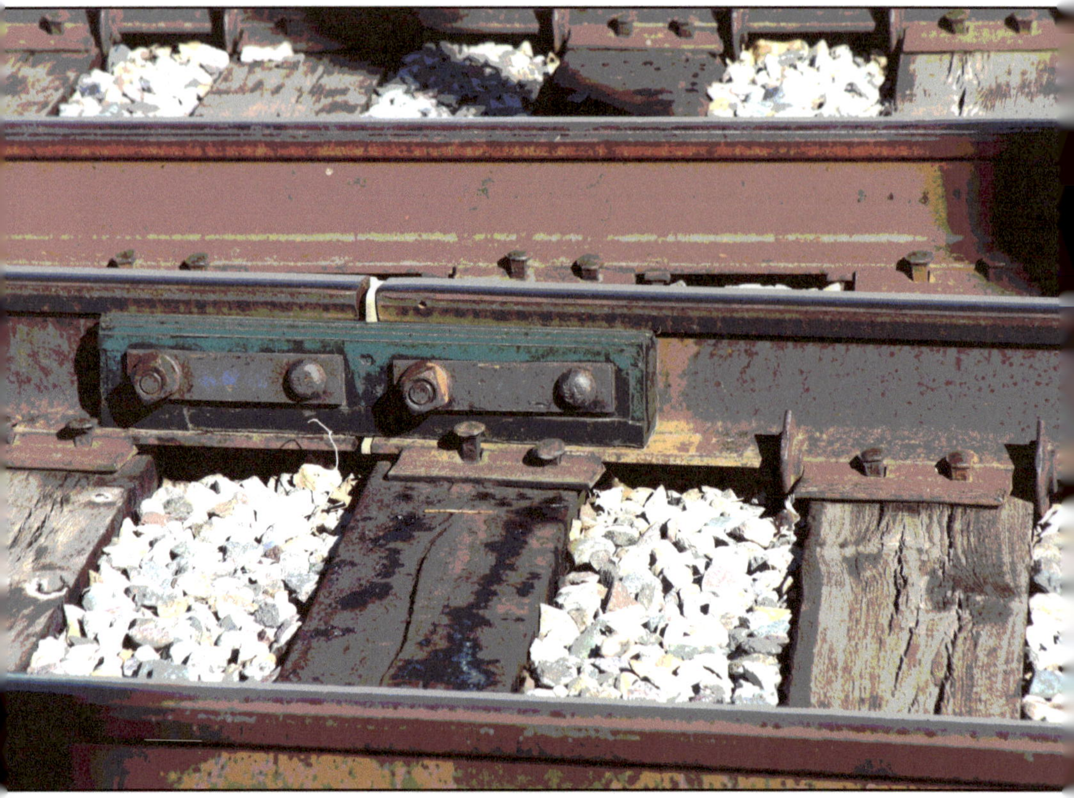

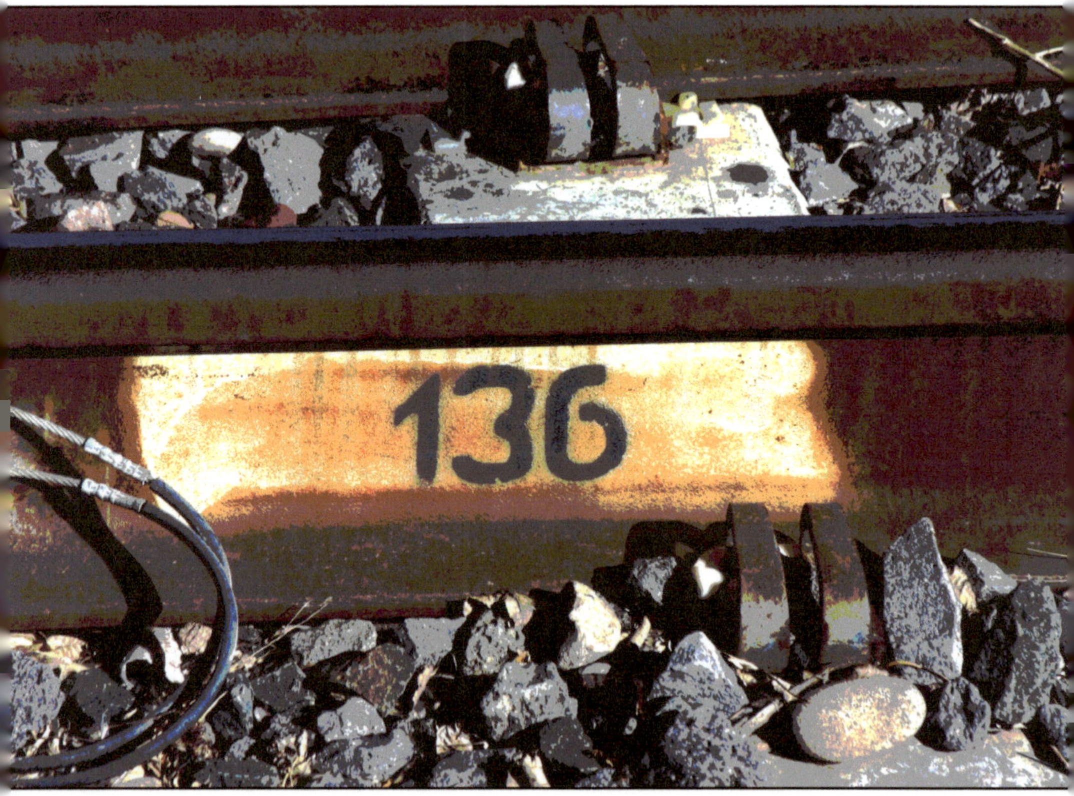

136

They'd practiced evacuations so many times he
knew she didn't mean ten o'clock. It was a code.
Ten meant – the HyperLoop was dulling his senses
and thinking was getting harder – ten meant . . .
it meant he had to get out of town. Immediately.
It was bad. They got key Senators out at nine. At
ten they erased the place where his dad worked.
The problem was bad enough to abandon decades
of research. He tried to focus. Ten meant his dad
might be dead. If his dad had been in Plant Nine
when it was erased, they would not have waited
for him to get out. He would just be an unfortunate
casualty. That was bad, too. He smiled. The drug
was kicking in so strong he couldn't feel bad about
anything. Level ten. He'd have to leave now, to go
with his mom, even if he was in trouble.

That was his last thought as he lost consciousness.

~~

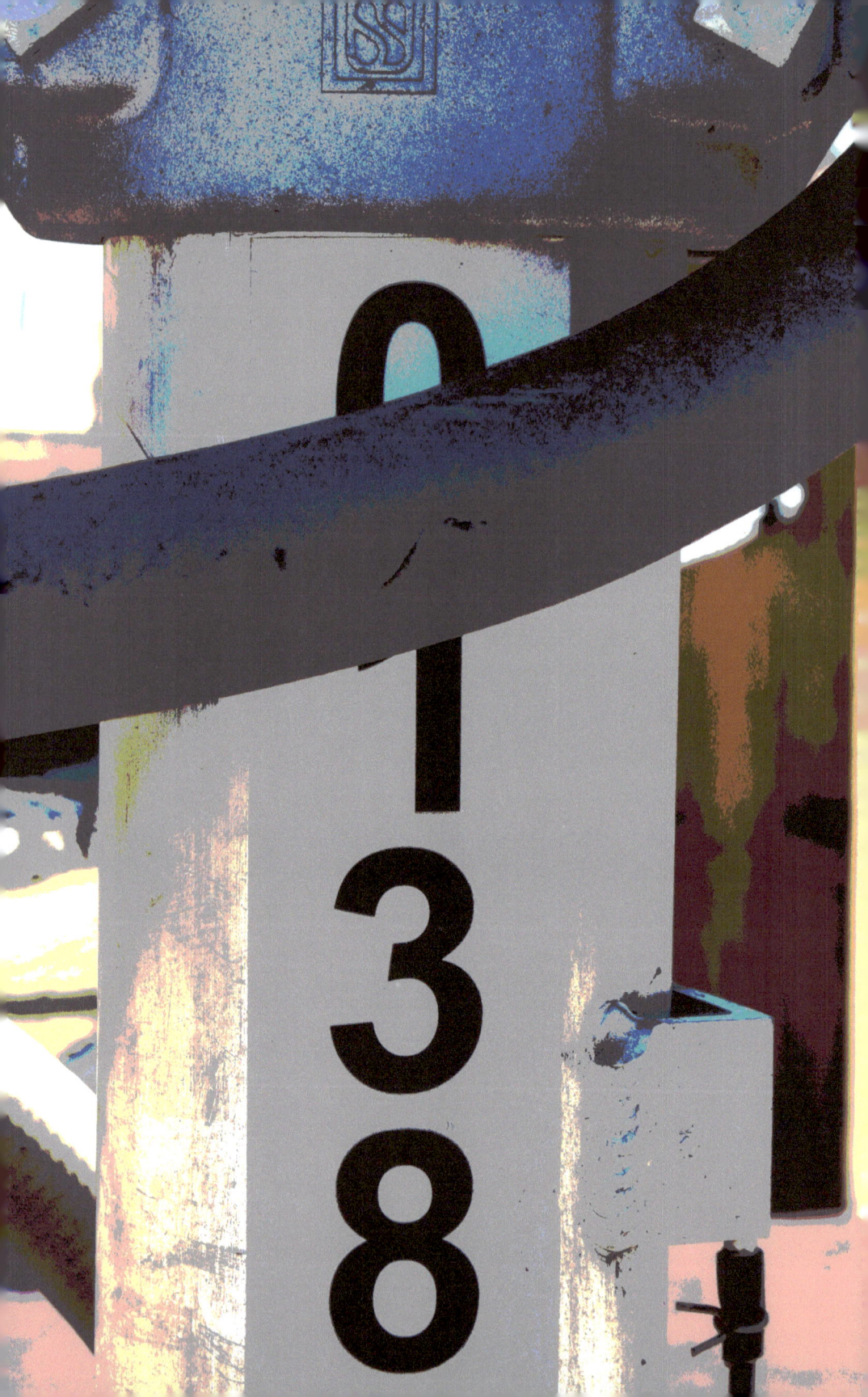

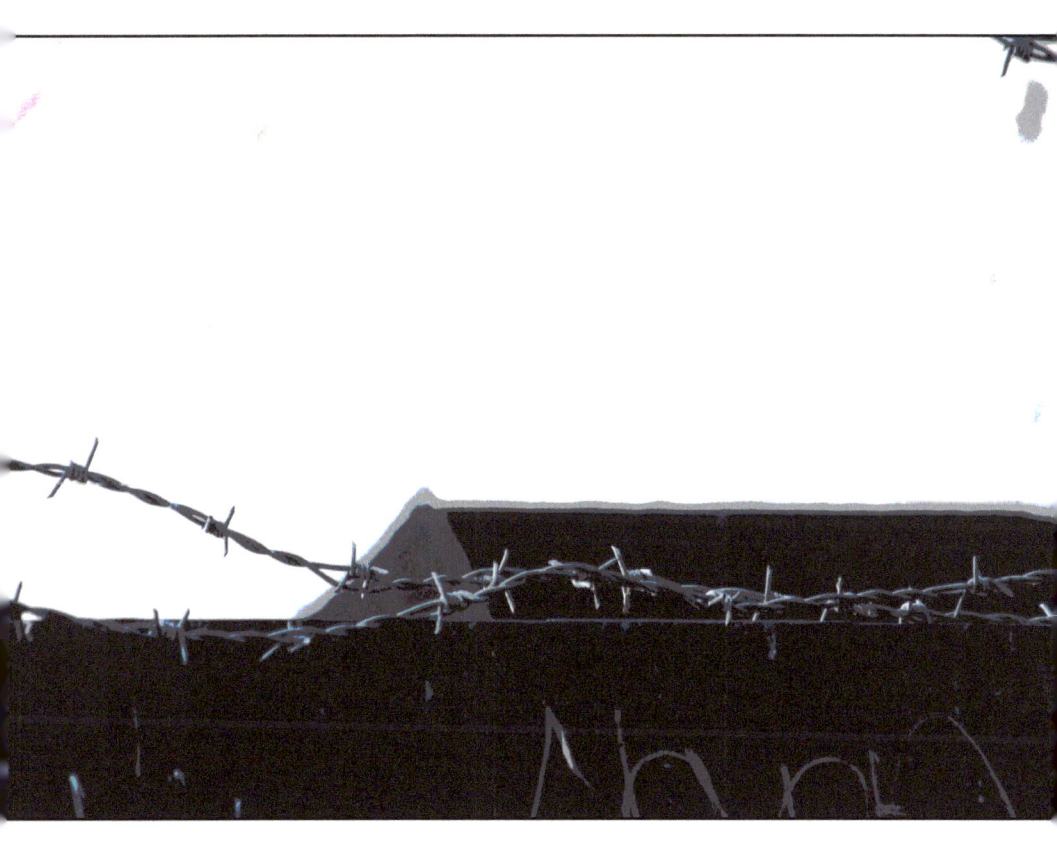

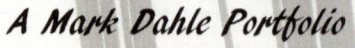

*A Mark Dahle Portfolio*

# Escape

**Present Divestment #6**

*This Mark Dahle Portfolio includes a colorful abstract painting, twenty-five gorgeous photographs from Florida, and a story about a family trying to escape disaster.*

Lisa pulled down her jacket and walked briskly into the entrance to the employment office. Earlier she had thought it would be easy to pick up her kids. Now she wondered if she had any chance at all to get her son. She had too much experience already with the Feast.

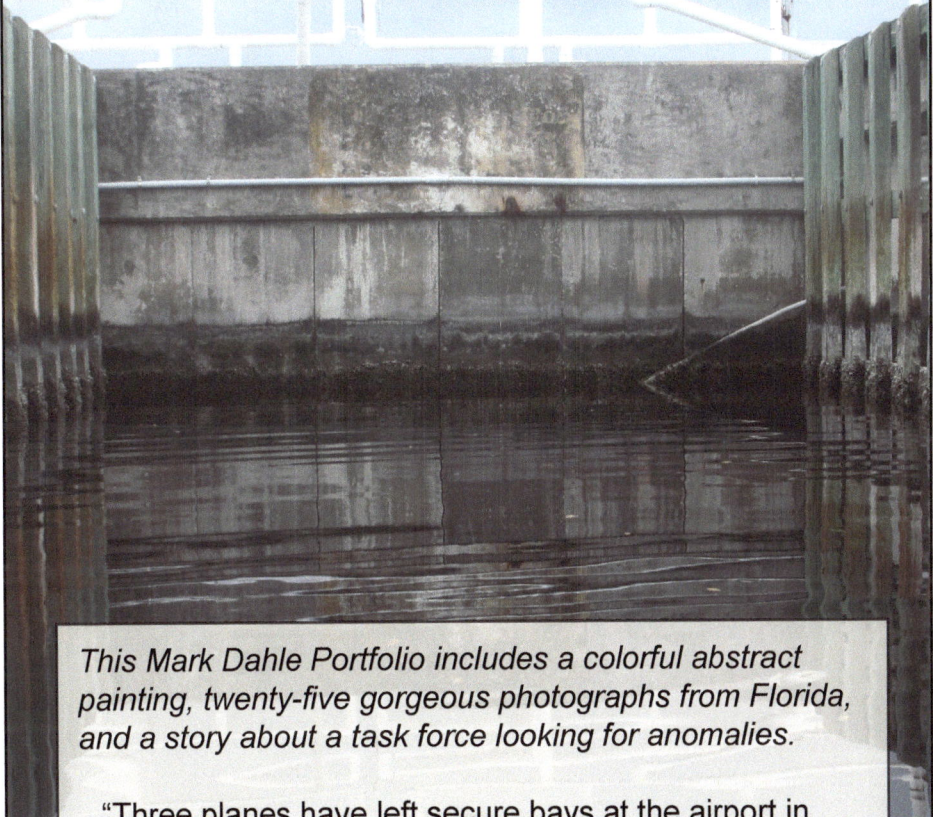

*A Mark Dahle Portfolio*

# Anomalies

## Present Divestment #7

*This Mark Dahle Portfolio includes a colorful abstract painting, twenty-five gorgeous photographs from Florida, and a story about a task force looking for anomalies.*

"Three planes have left secure bays at the airport in the past hour. Is there something I should know, sir?"

"I got a tip. I'm not sure the Corporation is really at level three. What anomalies have you seen today?"

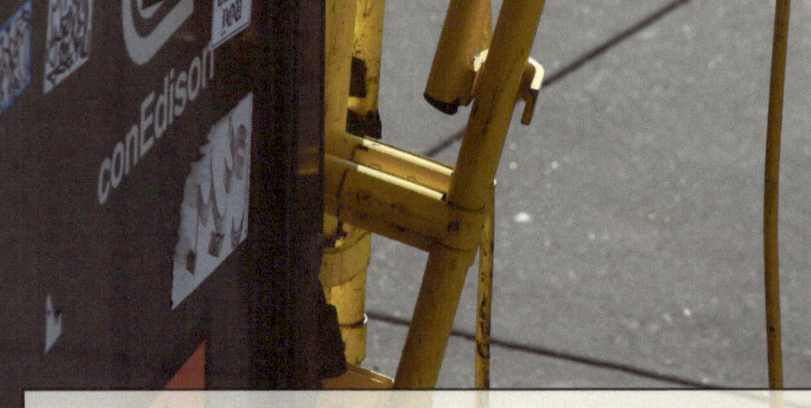

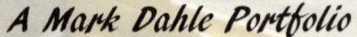

A Mark Dahle Portfolio

# Checking On Jarci

**Present Divestment #8**

*This Mark Dahle Portfolio includes a colorful abstract painting, twenty-five gorgeous photographs from Florida, and a story about a family trying to escape disaster.*

"Where is Jarci?"

"Her IdentiChip reports her location at her apartment. But she doesn't respond, sir. To anything."

www.ingramcontent.com/pod-product-compliance
Lightning Source LLC
Chambersburg PA
CBHW040858180526
45159CB00001B/460